SPORTS GOATs:
THE GREATEST OF ALL TIME

GOATs OF SOCCER

BY ANTHONY K. HEWSON

SportsZone

An Imprint of Abdo Publishing
abdobooks.com

abdobooks.com

Published by Abdo Publishing, a division of ABDO, PO Box 398166, Minneapolis, Minnesota 55439. Copyright © 2022 by Abdo Consulting Group, Inc. International copyrights reserved in all countries. No part of this book may be reproduced in any form without written permission from the publisher. SportsZone™ is a trademark and logo of Abdo Publishing.

Printed in the United States of America, North Mankato, Minnesota.
102021
012022

THIS BOOK CONTAINS
RECYCLED MATERIALS

Cover Photo: Joan Monfort/AP Images
Interior Photos: Zentralbild/picture-alliance/dpa/AP Images, 4, 5; Universal/Corbis/VCG/Getty Images, 6, 6–7; AP Images, 8, 8–9; Don Morley/Allsport/Getty Images, 10, 11; Rolf Kosecki/picture-alliance/dpa/AP Images, 12, 12–13; Roland Scheidemann/picture-alliance/dpa/AP Images, 14–15, 15; Colorsport/Shutterstock Images, 16, 16–17; Massimo Sambucetti/AP Images, 18, 19; Michael Probst/AP Images, 20, 20–21; John T. Greilick/AP Images, 22–23, 23; Ezra O. Shaw/Allsport/Getty Images Sport/Getty Images, 24–25, 25; Phil Cole/Getty Images Sport Classic/Getty Images, 26, 26–27; Markus Ullmer/picture-alliance/dpa/AP Images, 28, 28–29; Lars Baron/picture-alliance/dpa/AP Images, 30–31, 31; Naomi Baker/Getty Images Sport/Getty Images, 32, 32–33; Buda Mendes/Getty Images Sport/Getty Images, 34–35, 35; Lefteris Pitarakis/AP Images, 36, 36–37; Daniel Ochoa de Olza/AP Images, 38, 39; Bruna Prado/AP Images, 40, 40–41; Francisco Seco/AP Images, 42, 42–43

Editor: Charlie Beattie
Series Designer: Jake Nordby

Library of Congress Control Number: 2021941722

Publisher's Cataloging-in-Publication Data

Names: Hewson, Anthony K., author.
Title: GOATs of soccer / by Anthony K. Hewson
Description: Minneapolis, Minnesota : Abdo Publishing, 2022 | Series: Sports GOATs: The greatest of all time | Includes online resources and index.
Identifiers: ISBN 9781532196539 (lib. bdg.) | ISBN 9781644947135 (pbk.) | ISBN 9781098218348 (ebook)
Subjects: LCSH: Soccer--Juvenile literature. | European football--Juvenile literature. | Soccer--Records--Juvenile literature. | World Cup (Soccer)--Juvenile literature. | Professional athletes--Juvenile literature.
Classification: DDC 796.334--dc23

TABLE OF CONTENTS

FERENC PUSKÁS

Ferenc Puskás starred before soccer matches were widely available on television. Fans had to go see the striker play. Puskás made such an impression on fans that he became one of soccer's first international superstars.

In 1943 Puskás began his career with a club called Honved in his native Hungary. He played 13 years for Honved and averaged more than a goal per game. But Puskás really made his mark with his national team. Known as the "Mighty Magyars," the Hungarians were one of the best teams of the 1950s. And Puskás was their star. He scored two goals in a historic victory over world powerhouse England in 1953.

Puskás stood just 5 feet, 8 inches tall. But he was a powerful and speedy player. His left foot could deliver both a rocket shot and a precise pass. He led Hungary to the 1954 World Cup final, but they were surprisingly upset by West Germany.

His club career reached new heights when he joined Real Madrid in 1958. Puskás scored 242 goals in 262 matches. In the final of the 1960 European Cup—now known as the Champions League—Puskás scored three of his four goals in the second half and led Madrid to victory.

FAST FACT

Puskás is one of the few players who played in the World Cup for two different countries. He defected from Hungary in 1956 to get away from the country's communist government and settled in Spain. By 1962 he was a Spanish citizen and played for his new country at the 1962 World Cup.

Puskás died in 2006. In 2009 the Puskás Award was created. It is presented each year to the man or woman who scores the most beautiful goal of the season, meaning that Puskás's name will forever be associated with the kind of incredible goals that made him famous.

Ferenc Puskás scored 84 times in 85 appearances for the Hungarian national team.

LEV YASHIN

Lev Yashin had many nicknames during his career in the 1950s and 1960s. Some called him the Black Panther. Others called him the Black Spider. Many still call him the greatest goalkeeper of all time.

Any of those nicknames apply to Yashin. He always wore a dark uniform. He moved quickly like a jungle cat. Opposing players might have mistaken him for an eight-limbed spider, as he seemed to cover the entire goal. Yashin was especially known for saving penalties. He stopped an estimated 150 in his career.

Playing for his hometown club Dynamo Moscow as well as the Soviet national team, Yashin changed the position. He was one of the first goalkeepers to charge out of his goal to stop shots. And he used his booming voice to shout instructions to his entire team.

Perhaps Yashin's greatest moment came in the 1960 European Championship. He allowed only one goal in two matches as the Soviet Union won its first European title. Yashin also played in four World Cups. However, a poor performance at the 1962 World Cup caused fans to ask for his retirement.

Yashin responded with his best season yet. In 1963 he allowed just seven goals in 27 matches for Dynamo. At the end of the year, he won the Ballon d'Or, presented to the best soccer player in the world. Nearly 60 years later, he remained the only goalkeeper to ever win it.

FAST FACT

Yashin led the Soviets to the gold medal at the 1956 Olympic Games. He conceded only two goals in four games.

Lev Yashin played in three World Cups for the Soviet Union.

PELÉ

ew players make their World Cup debut at the age of 17. Even fewer score a goal. Pelé scored six when he debuted at the 1958 tournament in Sweden. And he did it in just three games.

After missing the first half of the tournament due to an injury, the Brazilian attacker scored the winner in the quarterfinals against Wales. He then delivered a hat trick against France. The boy wonder scored two more goals in the final to boost Brazil to its first World Cup title. The legend of Pelé was just getting started. He would play in three more World Cups with Brazil and win two of them.

The player born Edson Arantes do Nascimento was already a star in his native Brazil by 1958. Playing for legendary club Santos, Pelé averaged more than a goal per game. But the 1958 World Cup made him an international celebrity.

Pelé called soccer the "Beautiful Game." He played with a style and flair not seen before. Pelé was known as a great dribbler who could shoot with either foot. And he did more than just score. Pelé was also a skillful passer with great vision. He was involved in more than half of Brazil's 19 goals at his last World Cup in 1970.

He left Brazil in 1975 for a new league in North America. While playing for the New York Cosmos, he helped make soccer more popular in the United States. Pelé scored his final goal in front of 75,000 New York fans on October 1, 1977. It was the last of more than 1,000 goals in his decorated career.

Pelé is carried off the field by Brazilian fans after winning the 1970 World Cup in Mexico. He had four goals in six tournament matches, including one in the final against Italy.

BOBBY CHARLTON

Manchester United fans have seen many great players at the famous club through the years. None is a bigger hero to them than Bobby Charlton. After making his debut with the club as a teenager in 1956, the midfielder played more than 750 matches in the team's iconic red shirt. He scored nearly 250 goals.

Thrilling fans with his ball skills and booming shot, Charlton helped United win the English league title in his first season. But he is best remembered for leading the club through its darkest hour.

United was returning from a 1958 match in Yugoslavia when the team plane crashed in Munich, West Germany. Eight of the 16 players on board died. Two others never played again. Charlton survived and stuck with the club as it rebuilt. In 1963 United won the FA Cup, England's largest tournament, which features teams from all levels of soccer.

Charlton's greatest triumph was still ahead of him. In 1966 he became a hero for all of England. The country hosted the 1966 World Cup. Charlton's thundering goal in the team's second match had fans believing they could win the tournament for the first time. And they did, knocking off West Germany 4–2 in the final. Charlton was awarded the Ballon d'Or that year.

FAST FACT

Charlton's older brother Jack played for Leeds United in England. For a while, both Bobby and Jack held the career appearances record for each of their clubs.

He played a midfield role that required him to mark star players and make tackles. But Charlton received only two cautions, the equivalent of a yellow card today, in his long career. He retired from the English national team with a record 106 caps in 1970.

Bobby Charlton controls the ball for Manchester United in a 1973 match against Chelsea.

FRANZ BECKENBAUER

Franz Beckenbauer started out as a midfielder. But it was in defense that he became one of the greatest players of all time. Beckenbauer was known as *Der Kaiser*—"the Emperor." He brought his midfield skills to the back line, changing the center back position forever.

After making his professional debut with Bayern Munich in 1964, Beckenbauer helped the club win promotion into Germany's top league. Shortly after becoming captain in 1968, Beckenbauer began playing more in defense. Defenders at the time hardly ever participated in attacks. But Beckenbauer often made runs up the field and contributed on offense.

In this role, Beckenbauer was known as a "sweeper." With the ball at his feet, he could unleash dangerous curling shots. When he was defending, he could shut down the best goal scorers in the world.

Beckenbauer's career reached new heights as a sweeper. He led Bayern to three league titles in a row from 1972 to 1974. He also took West Germany back to the top while captaining the national side. First they won the European Championship in 1972. No team had ever won the European title and the World Cup back-to-back. Beckenbauer's West Germany completed the feat, knocking off a powerful Dutch team in the final of the 1974 World Cup, 2–1. The match was played on West Germany's home soil in Munich.

In 1972 and 1976, Beckenbauer won the Ballon d'Or. He was the first defender ever to win it. And he remains the only defender to have won it twice.

Franz Beckenbauer holds up the FIFA World Cup trophy after West Germany's 2–1 victory over the Netherlands in 1974.

Johan Cruyff of the Netherlands recovers the ball in time to score after gliding past the Argentine goalkeeper during the 1974 World Cup second round.

JOHAN CRUYFF

A new style of play came out of the Netherlands in the 1960s. It was called "Total Football." To execute it, every player needed to be able to switch positions. They also had to be skilled with the ball. It was a perfect fit for a player like Johan Cruyff.

Cruyff was one of the most creative players in soccer history. Technically he was a center forward. But Cruyff would pop up everywhere on the field. Defenders struggled to keep track of him.

The Total Football system was invented at Cruyff's club, Ajax. From 1971 to 1973, the Amsterdam-based club won three European Cups in a row. Cruyff took home two Ballon d'Or awards in that stretch.

The following World Cup, in 1974, was special for both Cruyff and the Dutch national team. Cruyff was everywhere at the tournament. He scored or assisted on eight of the team's 15 goals during its run to the final. At the end of the year, Cruyff was awarded his third Ballon d'Or.

It was at the World Cup that Cruyff unveiled what would become his most famous move. Against Sweden, Cruyff acted like he was about to kick the ball. But at the last second, he dragged the ball behind his other leg and ran away with it. The "Cruyff Turn" is still widely used today.

Cruyff eventually left Ajax to play professionally in Spain with Barcelona. He then spent three years in the United States before returning to the Netherlands at the end of his career. He remains a hero in his home country. Ajax renamed its home field Johan Cruyff Arena following his death from cancer in 2016.

MICHEL PLATINI

Some of the most beloved artists in history came from France. Michel Platini could be considered one of them. Instead of paint or clay, Platini made art out of free kicks.

Platini was a spectacular all-around attacker. But he was best known for his well-placed free kicks. The free kick has always been an important part of soccer. When Platini took one, it could be deadly.

Platini was known simply as *Le Roi*—"the King." After starting his club career in France, he moved to Juventus in 1982. With the Italian giants, Platini reached new levels of success. He won the Ballon d'Or three years in a row from 1983 to 1985.

A midfielder, Platini could score like a forward. At the 1984 European Championship, Platini scored a tournament-record nine goals in five matches. He scored hat tricks in back-to-back games against Belgium and Yugoslavia.

His eighth and ninth goals of the tournament were both game-winners. In the semifinals against Portugal, he finished a team attack in the 119th minute for a dramatic 3–2 victory.

The finals against Spain were scoreless in the 57th minute. Platini had a free kick just outside the penalty area. He curled it around the Spanish wall, and it was mishandled by the goalkeeper before trickling over the line. France won the match 2–0 for its first major tournament title.

Platini retired suddenly in 1987. He was just 32, but his 41 international goals were the most of any French player at the time. His achievements set the standard for the next generation of French players.

Michel Platini reacts to scoring a goal during France's 2–0 victory over Italy at the 1986 World Cup in Mexico.

DIEGO MARADONA

Diego Maradona stood just 5 feet, 5 inches tall. But he was larger than life to fans around the world. The attacking midfielder was especially beloved in his native Argentina, where he became a national hero.

Soon after Maradona made his pro debut at 15 years old in 1976, opponents learned to fear him. He was a magical dribbler. Defenders struggled to take the ball from him. His nimble, powerful legs helped Maradona dart his way through defenses. His dribbling skills combined with excellent goal-scoring ability made him nearly impossible to stop.

Maradona was considered the world's best player by 1982. And when he moved to Europe with Barcelona, fans and media followed him everywhere. After two years in Spain, Maradona moved to Italy to play with Napoli and won two league titles.

But the legend of Maradona reached its peak in 1986. As captain of the Argentine national team, Maradona carried his country to the World Cup title. He also provided one of the World Cup's most enduring highlights.

FAST FACT

Before his "Goal of the Century" against England, Maradona scored another goal in the match that appeared to go in off his hand. When asked about the incident, Maradona said he scored the goal, "a little with his head, and a little with the hand of God." The infamous tally became forever known as the "Hand of God" goal, and Argentina won the match 2–1.

In the quarterfinals against England, Maradona received a pass in his own half, weaved through several flailing English defenders, and scored. It was the perfect display of Maradona's speed, dribbling, and finishing. The goal was later voted "Goal of the Century."

Maradona led a controversial and troubled life off the field, but he remained a hugely popular figure. When he died in 2020, Argentina went into three days of mourning. Soccer fans around the world who saw him play all held on to memories of his on-field brilliance.

Diego Maradona celebrates with Napoli fans after leading the club to its first-ever Serie A title in 1987.

ROBERTO BAGGIO

Historically the best playmaker on a soccer team wears uniform No. 10. The best goal scorer wears No. 9. Roberto Baggio was both on every team he played for. France legend Michel Platini once called him a "No. 9 and a half."

Baggio was so loved in Italy that even his hair had a nickname. He was known as *Il Divino Codino*—"the Divine Ponytail." But it wasn't just his style that fans admired. Baggio could play all over the field. He was creative at making passes and aggressive in running at defenders. Fans loved his spirit and passion, even though his brash personality sometimes led to conflicts with his coaches.

He starred for six different Italian clubs, including Juventus, AC Milan, and Inter Milan. When he retired in 2004, he was one of the highest scorers in Italian league history. But Baggio was most revered by Italian fans for what he did with the national team.

In 16 World Cup matches, Baggio scored nine times. That tied the record for the most in Italian history. He starred as Italy reached the 1990 semifinals on home soil. And in 1994, he scored five goals in three knockout-round matches as Italy reached the final.

The low point of Baggio's career came in that final. Needing to score to keep his team alive in the penalty shootout against Brazil, he missed Italy's final penalty. But that did not define Baggio's career. He returned to the tournament in 1998 and became the first Italian to score in three different World Cups. In 2011 he was the first-ever inductee into the Italian Football Hall of Fame.

Roberto Baggio celebrates his goal for Italy against Bulgaria during the 1994 World Cup semifinals in East Rutherford, New Jersey.

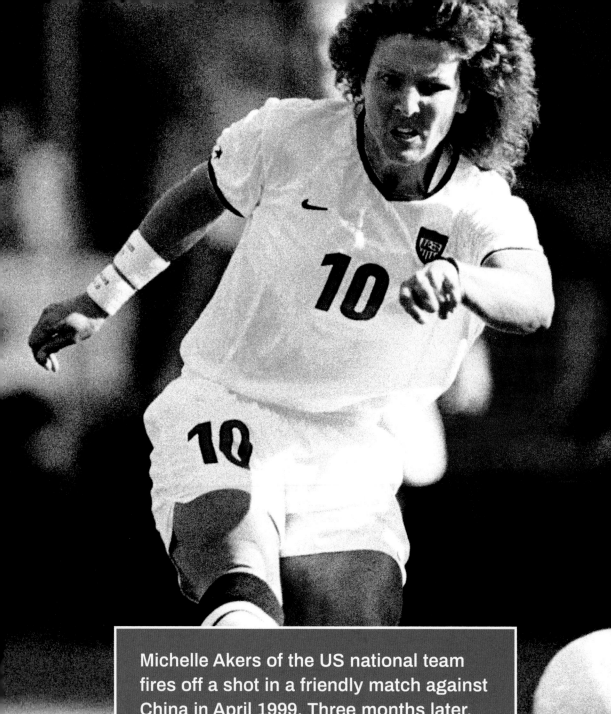

Michelle Akers of the US national team fires off a shot in a friendly match against China in April 1999. Three months later, the two teams would meet in the World Cup finals, with the US coming out on top in a penalty shootout.

MICHELLE AKERS

In many ways, the history of women's soccer in the United States began with Michelle Akers. Akers was on the first-ever US women's national team in 1985. On August 21 of that year, she scored the first goal in team history.

Few players have seen their sport change over the course of their careers as much as Akers did. Until 1991 there was not an official World Cup for women. Playing at forward, Akers was the star of that first tournament. She piled up 10 goals in six matches. That total included both goals in the final as the United States was crowned the first World Cup champion in women's soccer history.

Akers gave her team a burst of energy when she played. Her aggressive runs were instantly recognizable. Defenses struggled to stop her.

Akers also played a key role in the Olympic debut of women's soccer in 1996. Held on home soil in Athens, Georgia, the United States became the first gold medalist.

By that time, Akers was dealing with multiple injuries. She also suffered from chronic fatigue syndrome which could leave her exhausted. But Akers pressed on. The 1999 World Cup was held on home soil, and huge crowds came out to cheer on the team. Akers switched positions to defensive midfielder. Her role proved key to the team's success. She even added a goal in the semifinals against Brazil. Akers had to come out of the final after 91 minutes due to exhaustion but was able to rejoin her teammates after the match for the victory celebration.

Mia Hamm celebrates after scoring against Russia in 1998. The goal brought her tally to 101 in international play.

MIA HAMM

Mia Hamm was not women's soccer's first great player. But she was soccer's first female superstar. At the peak of her career in the late 1990s, screaming fans followed her wherever she went. The US striker delighted crowds of young soccer fans who wanted to be just like her.

It wasn't hard to see why. Hamm scored goals in bunches. She also won everywhere she played. The University of North Carolina won four straight college titles with Hamm on campus from 1989 to 1993. In between she scored twice to help the US national team win its first World Cup in 1991.

As the main goal scorer and face of the national team during the explosion of women's sports in the 1990s, Hamm became a nationwide celebrity. She was featured on magazine covers and in television commercials with other famous athletes like Michael Jordan.

Hamm cemented her greatness during the 1999 World Cup. She scored goals in the team's first two matches and added a pair of key assists. Her last act in the tournament came during the shootout in the final. Hamm calmly finished her kick to put the United States up 4–3 over China. Two kicks later, the US team was the champion again.

Hamm was only 15 when she first played for the national team in 1987. At the time she retired in 2004, her 158 international goals were the most of any player, male or female. Nearly two decades later, she still ranked third.

ZINEDINE ZIDANE

By skill alone, Zinedine Zidane was one of the most graceful soccer players ever. The midfielder was a magician with the ball. Creativity and vision came naturally. At 6 feet, 1 inch tall, he was also physically imposing on the field.

What made him an icon was his play in the biggest moments. That showed in the 1998 World Cup. With France hosting, Zidane led the home team to the final. Then his two headed goals helped France beat Brazil to win its first World Cup. Four years later, he was in the spotlight again. His club, Real Madrid, was playing Bayer Leverkusen in the Champions League final. Late in the first half of a 1–1 tie, Zidane drilled a spectacular volley from the top of the box. The ball rocketed into the top corner of the net. Real Madrid won the match 2–1. A 2020 poll voted it the most beautiful goal in Champions League history.

Zidane played for some of the biggest clubs in the world. He moved from Bordeaux in France to Juventus in 1996 and later to Real Madrid. The Spanish giants paid a record price to get him. Zidane lived up to the large price tag. He was voted FIFA World Player of the Year three times.

Zidane retired after leading France to the final of the 2006 World Cup. He later became a successful manager and led Real Madrid to a record three Champions League victories in a row from 2016 to 2018.

In France he was a national hero. Zidane was awarded the Legion of Honour in 1998. It is the highest award a French citizen can receive.

FAST FACT

Zidane could sometimes be undisciplined. He received 14 red cards in his career. Many people's lasting memory of Zidane was when he received a red card for headbutting an opponent in the 2006 World Cup final.

Zinedine Zidane (10) is mobbed by a pair of French teammates after scoring against Poland in 2000.

RONALDO

For many fans around the world, no player can ever match the greatness of Pelé. In the 1990s, another Brazilian striker emerged. Ronaldo made many fans in Brazil think they were seeing the next Pelé.

Ronaldo Luis Nazario de Lima was a classic striker. He had all the physical tools teams look for in a forward. His quick feet controlled the ball in tight spaces. Ronaldo was able to turn and weave through defenders or simply use his speed to go around them.

As a 17-year-old in 1994, Ronaldo was part of Brazil's World Cup-winning team but did not play in any matches. By 1996 he was FIFA World Player of the Year, and he was still only 20. He would win the award two more times in his career.

At the 1998 World Cup, Ronaldo was Brazil's star. He scored four times in the tournament, but Brazil came up short against host France in the final. Ronaldo played poorly against France, but news later emerged that he had suffered a seizure the morning of the match. Ronaldo was still awarded the Golden Ball as the tournament's best player.

His chance at redemption came four years later. After missing most of Brazil's World Cup qualifying games through injury, he returned just in time to score eight goals in seven games at the tournament held in South Korea and Japan. The 25-year-old scored twice in the final against Germany as Brazil lifted the FIFA World Cup trophy once again.

In 2006 he scored three more World Cup goals to bring his total up to 15 at the tournament. It was a record at the time. By then the comparisons to Pelé did not seem so outrageous.

Ronaldo celebrates one of his two goals against Germany at the 2002 World Cup final in Yokohama, Japan.

Birgit Prinz receives applause from both teams as she leaves the field after her final appearance for the German national team.

BIRGIT PRINZ

It was clear from her first game that Birgit Prinz was going to be a difference maker for Germany's national team. Prinz made her international debut as a 16-year-old in 1994. She scored the game-winning goal in the 89th minute.

After that Prinz became a key member of the national team. She became one of the first superstars of women's soccer. With Prinz, Germany won five European Championship tournaments, three Olympic medals, and two World Cups. She made more appearances for Germany than any other player.

A forward, Prinz was a fast and powerful runner. At 5 feet, 10 inches tall, she had a long stride. She was also stronger than what defenders were used to. Teams struggled to defend her.

Prinz simply scored goals. A true striker, she scored 128 in 214 international appearances. At one point, she held the record for most goals at both the World Cup and the Olympic Games.

In 2003 Prinz led Germany to its first World Cup title. The same year, she won her first of three consecutive FIFA World Player of the Year awards. Through 2020 only one player had won more. In 2007 Prinz drilled a long-range goal in the final that secured Germany's second consecutive World Cup title.

Prinz remained a productive player into her early 30s. She played in her fifth and final World Cup in 2011 before retiring.

CHRISTINE SINCLAIR

Great players in successful soccer countries inspire fans by winning championships. In Canada Christine Sinclair took a country that struggled in soccer and made it a champion.

Sinclair debuted for Canada at the Algarve Cup in 2000. She was just 16 years old. Up to that point, the Canadians weren't winning many matches. They had never qualified for the Olympics, and they didn't record a win at either the 1995 or 1999 World Cup. But when the striker from Burnaby, British Columbia, scored in her second career match, Canada's fortunes started to change. They finished fourth at the 2003 World Cup with Sinclair leading the way.

Sinclair scored goals at a record pace. She tallied the first of her 10 career World Cup goals just four minutes into her first match in 2003. And she was even better at the Olympic Games. Sinclair scored a record six at the 2012 games in London. That total included a sensational hat trick against the favored United States in the semifinals. Canada lost the match, 4–3, but went home with the bronze medal. For her efforts, Sinclair was chosen to carry Canada's flag at the closing ceremonies.

They took bronze again in 2016, with Sinclair still piling up goals into her thirties. By 2019 she had tied Abby Wambach's record of 184 international goals. She broke the record on January 29, 2020.

At Tokyo 2020, Sinclair and Canada had another chance at Olympic glory. Sinclair was 38 years old and teamed with players she had inspired to take up the game. She scored her only goal in the opening match against Japan, but her leadership carried Canada through as they topped Sweden for the nation's first-ever major tournament victory.

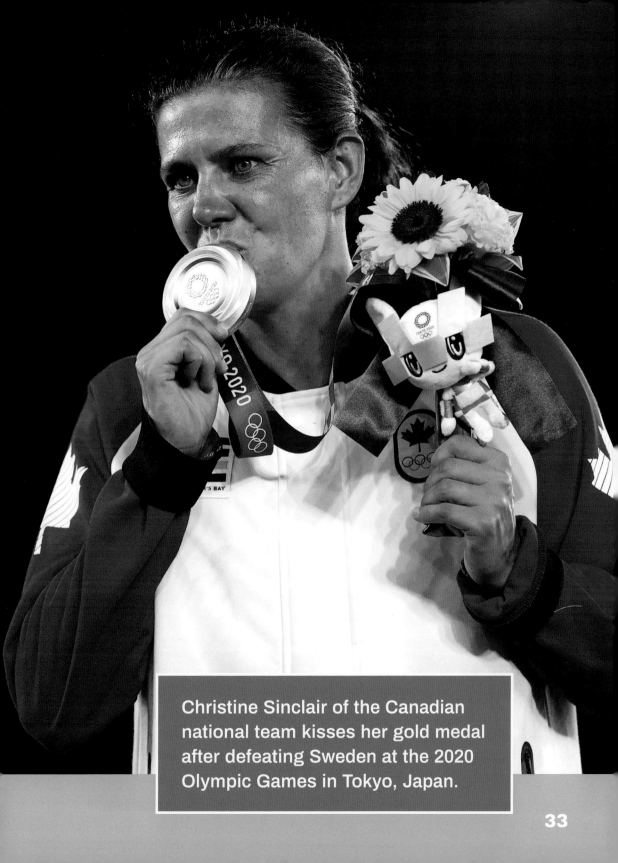

Christine Sinclair of the Canadian national team kisses her gold medal after defeating Sweden at the 2020 Olympic Games in Tokyo, Japan.

Marta fires up the crowd at Rio de Janeiro's famous Maracana Stadium after converting a penalty during the 2016 Olympic semifinals against Sweden.

MARTA

Many young players have been compared to Pelé. Not many have received that comparison by Pelé himself. But indeed Pelé once identified a young Brazilian forward who had technical ability and speed just like he did. Her name was Marta.

Marta grew up playing soccer like many Brazilian kids do. They play on the streets using whatever equipment is available. Playing in scrappy games like those helped Marta develop her technical ability and toughness.

By the age of 17, she scored three goals for Brazil at the 2003 World Cup. That marked the first of five World Cups she played in. Her 17 World Cup goals through 2019 were a record.

In addition to scoring goals, she helped Brazil finally achieve success at major tournaments. The team took home silver at the 2004 Olympics in Athens, Greece, and at the 2008 Games in Beijing, China. In between Brazil finished second at the 2007 World Cup. Marta won the tournament's Golden Ball award for best player and Golden Boot award for top scorer.

Marta has dazzling ability with the ball at her feet. Fellow players marvel at her ability to control the ball without losing speed. She can play in a variety of roles. And she plays with a style and passion like many other top Brazilian players.

In 2006 she won her first of five consecutive World Player of the Year awards. She added a sixth in 2018. At that time, no other player had more than three.

ABBY WAMBACH

When legends like Michelle Akers and Mia Hamm left the US national team in the early 2000s, it was time for a new generation of stars. Abby Wambach was ready to lead the way. She did it by scoring goals—a lot of them.

Wambach made her national team debut in 2001. Despite making only fourteen appearances before the 2003 World Cup, she impressed enough to make the team. She then scored three goals in six matches.

Unlike some high-scoring forwards, Wambach was not especially fast or flashy. Her best attribute was her ability to win aerial battles. At 5 feet, 11 inches tall, she was a physical presence in the box.

That ability led to one of the most dramatic goals in soccer history. In the 122nd minute of the 2011 World Cup quarterfinals against Brazil, the United States was trailing 2–1. From the far sideline, US winger Megan Rapinoe hurled a deep cross toward the back post. Wambach was there to power it home with her head. It was the latest goal ever scored in a World Cup match. The United States eventually won on penalties.

The US team failed to win that tournament. But Wambach helped put them back on top in 2015. She scored her fourteenth World Cup goal in the final group game. The US women went on to defeat Japan in the final. Wambach retired after the tournament. At the time, her 184 goals were an international record. The number still stands as a US record.

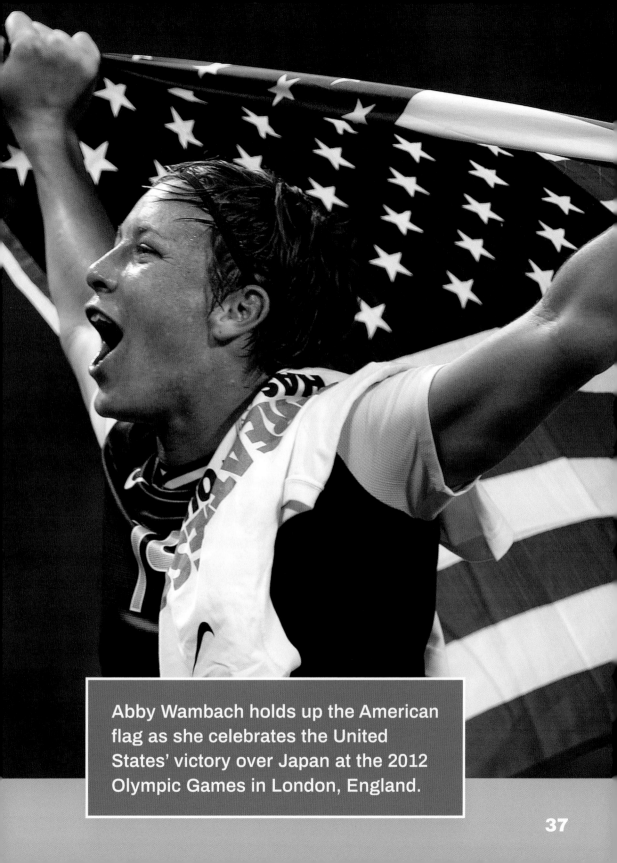

Abby Wambach holds up the American flag as she celebrates the United States' victory over Japan at the 2012 Olympic Games in London, England.

CRISTIANO RONALDO

Cristiano Ronaldo was born and raised on Madeira, an island hundreds of miles off the coast of Portugal. That didn't stop the world's greatest clubs from noticing him. In 2003 Ronaldo was an 18-year-old playing for Sporting CP in Lisbon, Portugal, when England's Premier League came calling. Legendary Manchester United manager Sir Alex Ferguson called Ronaldo one of the most exciting players he had ever seen.

Ferguson was right. Ronaldo would go on to win five FIFA World Player of the Year awards. After winning his first with Manchester United in 2008, he added four more after a 2009 move to Real Madrid. He also won the Champions League four times with the Spanish giants. In 2021, after spending three seasons in Italy with Juventus, Ronaldo returned to Manchester United at the age of 36. He was still a star.

There are many reasons for Ronaldo's success. He is tall, athletic, and quick. Ronaldo can beat opponents in the air or burst past them with his speed. He delights crowds with his signature step-over dribbles.

Ronaldo also has a knack for dramatic goals. And he doesn't just score them for his club teams. In the summer of 2021, his five goals at the European Championship gave him 109 on his career, tying the

FAST FACT

In 2017 the Portuguese government named the airport on Ronaldo's home island of Madeira after him.

all-time men's international record. Portugal's next match was a World Cup qualifying game against Ireland in September. With his team trailing 1–0 in the 89th minute, Ronaldo powered a header into the bottom corner of the net to tie the game and claim the record.

And he wasn't done. In the sixth minute of stoppage time, another Ronaldo header won the match in dramatic fashion. His 111th international goal was the latest in a long career filled with spectacular moments.

Cristiano Ronaldo roars in celebration after scoring for Real Madrid against Bayern Munich during a 2012 Champions League semifinal match.

LIONEL MESSI

From the very beginning, Lionel Messi was compared to Diego Maradona. Both men hailed from Argentina. Both were shorter than average. Both had dazzling playmaking skills. And both were expected to lead their nation to glory.

The legend of Messi began in his hometown of Rosario, Argentina. He and his youth team lost just one game in four years. But Messi had been diagnosed with a growth disorder at age nine. He needed expensive hormone treatments to keep growing. Without them he would never be big enough to withstand a professional career.

Spanish giant Barcelona agreed to pay for Messi's treatments if he signed with them. So in 2000, at the age of 13, he moved to Spain. And he grew to 5 feet, 7 inches, two inches taller than Maradona.

Soon the goals started to pile up. Messi made his senior debut in 2004. Over the next 17 years, he racked up nearly 700 goals, scoring them in a variety of ways. He used his speed and dribbling ability to weave through defenses the way Maradona had. He could bend free kicks over and around nearly any defensive wall.

For all his club success, Messi struggled to bring home international glory for Argentina fans who were used to winning. Early in his career, Messi came close many times, including three runner-up finishes in the Copa América, South America's largest international tournament. Argentina was also runner up at the 2014 World Cup in Brazil.

In 2021 Messi finally achieved his championship moment. In seven Copa América matches, he scored four times and had five assists. After Argentina bested Brazil 1–0 in the final, his teammates carried Messi on their shoulders in celebration. His legacy was complete.

Surrounded by his teammates, Lionel Messi holds up the Copa América trophy after Argentina won the 2021 tournament.

MEGAN RAPINOE

Megan Rapinoe's international career got off to a delayed start. After making her debut with the US national team in 2006, injuries sidelined her for much of the next two years. But once she was healthy, Rapinoe became a key player for more than a decade.

Rapinoe showed off her talent as well as her big personality at the 2011 World Cup against Colombia. Seconds after she came on as a substitute, she unleashed a shot. After it beat the goalkeeper, she ran to a sideline microphone and sang Bruce Springsteen's "Born in the USA."

Rapinoe isn't afraid to show who she is on or off the field. On it the winger is a tricky player to defend. She has quick feet and can release passes to teammates or take bending shots on goal. Her creativity and playmaking ability elevate her teams.

Off the field, Rapinoe uses her platform as a world-class athlete to bring attention to several issues. She champions gay rights, social justice, and equal pay for women.

Rapinoe always made her mark whenever she played. After scoring in a quarterfinal win over France at the 2019 World Cup, Rapinoe's celebratory pose became an iconic image. She added a second goal later in the match, a 2–1 victory. Her six total goals tied teammate Alex Morgan and England's Ellen White for most in the tournament. And she helped the United States defend its World Cup title. Later that year, she won World Player of the Year for the first time.

FAST FACT

Rapinoe is one-half of one of the most accomplished athletic couples of all time. Her partner, WNBA star Sue Bird, has won four WNBA titles with the Seattle Storm and five Olympic gold medals in women's basketball.

Megan Rapinoe poses for the crowd after scoring her first goal during the 2019 World Cup quarterfinals against France.

HONORABLE
MENTIONS

ALFREDO DI STEFANO

The Argentine forward won the Ballon d'Or twice and helped Real Madrid win five consecutive European Cups in the 1950s and '60s.

EUSEBIO

The Portuguese speedster was a star striker for Benfica in the 1960s and '70s, scoring 317 times in 301 matches.

GERD MÜLLER

The prolific striker starred for West Germany at the 1974 World Cup. He retired as the highest-scoring player in World Cup history.

MARCO VAN BASTEN

Injuries shortened the Dutch forward's career in 1995 at age 30, but van Basten still scored 277 professional goals.

PAOLO MALDINI

The versatile Maldini was a defensive rock for AC Milan and the Italian national team for 24 years before retiring in 2009. He appeared 126 times for Italy, 74 as captain.

KRISTINE LILLY

Lilly earned 354 caps for the US national team, scoring 130 goals, before her retirement in 2010. She played in five World Cups and three Olympic Games.

HOMARE SAWA

Sawa captained Japan's women's national team to victory at the 2011 World Cup. A skilled playmaker, Sawa won World Player of the Year shortly after her World Cup triumph.

ANDRES INIESTA

A former Barcelona captain, Iniesta was a gifted playmaker who was key to Spain winning the 2008 European Championship. He then scored the winning goal in the 2010 World Cup final, Spain's only victory in tournament history.

GLOSSARY

assist
A pass that leads directly to a goal, or a rebound or deflection that leads to a goal.

Ballon d'Or
An award given out at the end of each year to the best male player in the world.

cap
A player's appearance in an international soccer game.

dribble
To control and advance the ball up the field with one's feet.

free kick
An unguarded kick awarded to a team after an opponent's foul.

header
A shot that involves striking the ball with one's head.

penalty shootout
A series of penalty kicks held if a game is tied after stoppage time to decide who wins.

red card
A card given to a player when they are ejected from the game for either playing violently or receiving two yellow cards.

volley
A ball that is kicked out of the air rather than from off the ground.

yellow card
A caution given to a player by a referee for playing dangerously or behaving badly.

MORE INFORMATION

BOOKS

Marthaler, Jon. *Ultimate Soccer Road Trip*. Minneapolis, MN: Abdo Publishing, 2019.

Nicks, Erin. *Cristiano Ronaldo*. Minneapolis, MN: Abdo Publishing, 2020.

Nicks, Erin. *Lionel Messi*. Minneapolis, MN: Abdo Publishing, 2020.

ONLINE RESOURCES

Booklinks
NONFICTION NETWORK
FREE! ONLINE NONFICTION RESOURCES

To learn more about the GOATs of soccer, please visit **abdobooklinks.com** or scan this QR code. These links are routinely monitored and updated to provide the most current information available.

INDEX

ABOUT THE AUTHOR

Anthony K. Hewson is a freelance writer originally from San Diego. He and his wife now live in the San Francisco Bay Area with their two dogs.